HOLDING ON TO THE VISION:

Defining and Fulfilling Your Divine Destiny

Inspired By: The Holy Spirit

Written By: Yolanda Grace Jones

authorHOUSE®

AuthorHouse™
1663 Liberty Drive
Bloomington, IN 47403
www.authorhouse.com
Phone: 1-800-839-8640

First published by AuthorHouse 10/13/2009

ISBN: 978-1-4490-2394-2 (sc)

Printed in the United States of America
Bloomington, Indiana

This book is printed on acid-free paper.

<u>Dedication:</u>

This book is dedicated to my beloved Pastor and Spiritual Mother, Dr. Minnie B. Washington. Thank you for your unconditional love, support, wisdom, and guidance through my journey in realizing and walking in my divine destiny. Your example of endless obedience to our Heavenly Father has taught me so much. Thank you for being my mentor, my mother, and my pastor.

May God bless you with an abundant harvest for all that you have sown in the lives of all of your children, (biological AND spiritual), and the saints of Tabernacle of Prayer Church. Passion for Christ Ministries could never have been birthed without God using you as His midwife.

FOREWARD

"…And He withdrew from them about a stone's throw, and He knelt down and began to pray:

'…Father, if you are willing, remove this cup from Me, yet not My will,

but Yours be done.'"

(Luke 22:41-42, NASB)

When I finished writing this book, the next step in its publication was to decide on an appropriate cover design. This is a step which I usually have covered before I finish the manuscript however this time would be different—*VERY* different! I meditated on the book's theme and ultimate message for days on end. I submitted a description of what I wanted for the cover. The publisher told me they could not produce it. I scanned hundreds of images on-line and selected what I felt was perfect—*again* the publisher denied my choice. By this time I was frustrated, angry, and ready to throw in the towel.

But I knew I could not do that—I was compelled to see this book released as God wanted, and obedience to His instruction was not up for discussion! I prayed for God's help (as I always do), because this was *His* message. Although He continues to use me as His vessel through which He conveys the wisdom for each book, my flesh always wants to get in the way and rush God!

There were so many ways I was tested along the way as this book was in process. The Spirit of God stirred me up each time I grew weary, and the passion and determination within me to complete it just would not go away. I felt convicted each time my flesh gave in to procrastination. Many days I asked myself (and God) why this assignment was so important—the devil would tell me things like, "It'll never happen—even if it does, no one will be interested in it anyway!" Our family endured personal tragedies like the death of my father, as well as the sudden death of my husband's father. Our financial situation began to really spiral downward. Stress and tension made it so hard to concentrate on anything other than what we were dealing with in the natural.

Yet as each day passed I felt God prodding me more and more about being obedient to His command. I wanted to run away from everything—including God! I spent days on my face, literally digging my nails and teeth into the carpet so not to back out on my mission. I prayed fervently for clarity on why this seemed so hard to accomplish. God answered:

> *"My child, this book is written for My people to understand the 'what, why, and how(s)' regarding their divine destiny. They must understand that the fulfillment of their destiny impacts the lives of others and the course of history in the future. Jesus, My Son, the Savior of the world was compelled to define and fulfill His destiny. He realized (or defined) His destiny at an early age, and spent years walking out the fulfillment of His destiny. There was much that He did and had to endure between the time He defined and ultimately sealed His purpose on the cross. If He had denied Me, if He had strayed along the way, and if His destiny had been aborted at the Garden of Gethsemane, there would be no hope for anyone to have access to Me, the Kingdom, or freedom from the grip of sin and death. Although that which you or other's have to endure in no way is comparable to My Son's sacrifice, His example set the course for you all to realize how vital My purpose is for your lives—I created all of mankind impregnated with a divine assignment which will impact the world. If you do not fulfill My assignment, the lives of others will be affected in a way contrary to My plan."*

After receiving the above revelation, I knew why the process and completion of this book was so vital. I also understood the tests and trials that accompanied the composition of this book. I pray that you all grasp God's words as I did. Jesus' birth, life, and price He rendered on Calvary are the epitome of the importance of our seeking God's wisdom, strength, grace, and guidance in fulfilling our individual God-given purpose. May our Heavenly Father speak to each of you personally as you read, receive, and digest each word on the message that follows…God bless!

Contents

INTRODUCTION

"For the vision is yet for the appointed time;

It hastens toward the goal and it will not fail.

Though it tarries, wait for it;

For it will certainly come, it will not delay."

(*Habakkuk 2:3, NASB*)

So often in our lives we ask ourselves, "Why am I here? What purpose do I have in this world?" Many of us ask these questions of God, and then spend years doing things which were never in His plan. As a result we live each day feeling unhappy, unfulfilled, and frustrated. There is an emptiness within that cannot be filled no matter how much money we have, or how many people we have around us that love us. It is a sad but true fact that so many go to their graves having not fulfilled their God-given destiny.

We must understand that God has a plan and purpose for us even before we come into this world. Indeed, when He forms us in our mother's womb He has a special design for our lives. This design is spoken over us by God and can only be revealed to us by Him. Some call this divine idea or "purpose" ordained by God, a vision. You may be saying to yourself, "I don't have a vision.", or maybe even "I already know my purpose and I'm still not happy!" Well if you've ever said or thought these things to yourself, I can tell you that you have been living under deception.

When God breathed life into you at your natural birth, He also implanted a "seed" which is sometimes called, "a dream". He also equipped you with the ability, or the tools you need to do that which He intended for you to accomplish in your life. I call it a "dream" because sometimes it is easier to identify and realize our purpose by using that term. Ask yourself,

"Is there something you want to do in your life that makes you excited when you think about it?" Is it something that comes natural and makes you feel so happy and fulfilled when you do it? Is it something that doesn't seem attainable with a great degree of success unless you have help or divine intervention? While you continue to perform a job or career that provides your natural needs, do you still long to be able to accomplish this "dream"? Is it something that won't go away no matter how long you go without thinking about it? If you have been able to identify something as I have been asking these questions, this, my friend, could be your divine purpose or vision.

If you have not yet realized your purpose, it will be revealed to you without a doubt. God discloses the vision for our lives often in very ordinary/simple ways. For me, it was a strong inner desire that just would not go away. I never really considered it to be a lifelong career because it seemed so impossible to achieve at the level of success needed for me to be able to depend on it to supply my material needs. In other words, I didn't see myself becoming successful enough at it to pay the bills!

But no matter how I tried, I couldn't get away from it. No matter how much I liked a job, it just wasn't enough to fulfill me. Over time I was becoming more and more frustrated because although I should have been happy, something was missing from my life. I had been blessed with a wonderful husband, two beautiful, healthy children, and everything I needed to be happy. But I still felt there was something more I was supposed to be doing with my life.

In the following pages, I would like to share with you some of the things God has shown me as I realized and began to walk in, my divine purpose. It is my sincere desire that after reading this book, you have not only identified your divine purpose/vision, but have been encouraged enough to step out of the boat and fulfill it.

1

The Conception - Against All Odds

"Behold, I will do something new,

Now it will spring forth;

Will you not be aware of it?"

(Isaiah 43:19, NASB)

In 1999, I was blessed by God to meet someone who would become not just my pastor, but who would adopt me as a spiritual daughter. Dr. Minnie B. Washington has been one of the most influential people God has used to nurture my walk with Him. She not only fostered my growth in the Word of God, but she lovingly guided and disciplined me as I began to walk in my divine purpose. She has been there to walk with me, and hold my hand in the early years.

She listened to many tearful conversations of me doubting the call on my life, as well as doubting where my life was going. She would always listen quietly, and end the call by saying "All is well, daughter, all is well." Many times I wanted to tell her "Mom, all is NOT well!!"

Dr. Washington knew when to let go of my hand, as every mother does when their child must learn to walk on their own. She never enabled me to remain dormant in my destiny. I learned so much under her tutelage—in fact, God is still using her in my life and in my ministry.

When I asked her to contribute to this book, she graciously agreed. Her wisdom and insight will bless you as it has blessed me. I asked her to share her testimony of how God birthed her ministry—the Holy Spirit carried her story far beyond. The remainder of this chapter is her words as the Spirit of God gave her utterance:

Life and service to God have more than one or two obstacles for you to have to overcome. The longer I live the more and more I have come to believe that it is something that burns in the heart of a man/woman that helps him/her to press on against the odds.

Jeremiah 29:11-13 (KJV) – "For I know the thoughts that I think toward you, saith the LORD, thoughts of peace, and not of evil, to give you an expected end. Then shall ye call upon me, and ye shall go and pray unto me, and I will hearken unto you. And ye shall seek me, and find me, when ye shall search for me with all your heart."

I must be dreaming! God are you saying I will give birth to another baby?! At MY age?! I have given birth to seven children, and the number seven is symbolic for divine completion. How could God now say I will give birth to another baby? I know the number eight is symbolic for new beginnings, but God I am passed the child bearing age! What are you saying to me?

Habakkuk 2:1 (KJV) – "And the LORD answered me, and said, write the vision, and make it plain upon tables, that he may run that readeth it."

*All of my life I've had to press on, against all odds. Throughout my entire life, I knew God was preparing me for something great. The preparation began according to **Jeremiah 1: 5 (KJV) – "Before I formed thee in the belly I knew thee; and before thou camest forth out of the womb I sanctified thee, and I ordained thee a prophet unto the nations. "***

My entire life was spent going to church; however when I was 39 years old and my youngest child was 13, my children asked me if I was saved. I had no clue what they were talking about! I was soon to learn about salvation and I accepted Jesus Christ as my Lord and Savior and subsequently was baptized with the Holy Spirit, thus began my odyssey of faith.

*From the year 1978 to present, I learned how to walk by faith and not by sight. No matter what my five senses told me I just walked by faith. **Hebrews 11:1 (KJV)** became prevalent in my life. It states, **"Now faith is the substance of things hoped for, the evidence of things not seen".** Hebrews 11:6 (KJV) states, **"But without faith it is impossible to please him: for he that cometh to God must believe that he is, and that he is a rewarder of them that diligently seek him".***

Against all odds, I diligently sought God day by day, month by month, and year by year. There were many struggles, hardships, trials and tribulations, but I continued my odyssey of faith. In 1987 God called me to the Gospel Ministry. Led by God, I made Virginia Beach, VA my home in July, 1990 and became a member of New Hope Baptist Church in 1992, where the odyssey of faith continued for 15 years. During that period of time, I subsequently was licensed and ordained to preach the gospel ministry.

Even though Virginia Beach, VA was my home, against all odds, I spent nine years in the District of Columbia where I was employed and attended Jericho Bible College and Washington Saturday College.

Against all odds, I worked hard, studied hard and subsequently obtained three academic degrees: Bachelor and Master Degrees in Religious Education and a Doctorate of Divinity Degree.

Against all odds, in 1990, the odyssey continued as I retired from my secular job which concluded 29 years at the Federal Government. Subsequently, the most exciting chapter of my life began a life of "Full Time Ministry" working for God, but also brought about the greatest struggles in my life.

God blessed my husband and me with a beautiful home which I still reside in. It was during the dedication of the home, amongst all of my children; family; neighbors; and friends God spoke and said, "This will always be a "House of Prayer for all people"; they will come to be refreshed through prayer and My Word, and then sent out renewed and refreshed with a new perspective on life. I will tell you how long they will say and what you are to speak to them".

However, against all odds, four years later God called my husband home to be with Him. After a year of traveling, spending time with my children, family and friends and grieving for my husband, God spoke and said, "It is now time to give birth to the House of Prayer for all people". As far as I was concerned, it had already been established.

However, as God referred me back to the vision He had given me, I knew it was much greater than my residence. God said it is now time to give birth to the baby I had carried for five years and it was to be named "Tabernacle of Prayer Church" (TOPC). As I wrestled back and forth with God; even at times trying to by-pass what He had called and gifted me to do, I must admit I attempted to bargain with God by starting a radio and internet ministry.

Against all odds, I began broadcasting the Word of God for 30 minutes daily on the radio However; it did not please God, because I began walking by sight and not by faith. My greatest fear, (even though I knew God did not give me a spirit of fear, but power, love and a sound mind,) was not pleasing God. I struggled with the idea of having conceived, or being impregnated with, this new baby which I often refer to as "Baby Tabernacle".

When God gives you a vision, and you know, that you know, that you know, it came directly from the throne room of God, often it is hard for others to understand or receive. However, God gave me a list of names of persons to share the vision with. God said "Don't worry about those who do not receive what I am doing. Many will say they are with you, but know that only those whom I have called to this ministry will believe and accept what I am doing". Even though I didn't have a clue of how to go about doing what God had spoken, step by step the Holy Spirit led and guided me. Even though all odds were against me, I learned to live by **Romans 8:28 KJV, "And we know that all things work together for good to them that love God, to them who are called according to his purpose."**

Against all odds, fellowship began at my home on January 1, 2006. Against all odds, TOPC was born on February 5, 2006, at the Central Library on Virginia Beach Blvd, Virginia Beach, where over 100 persons were in attendance. The message God gave me for the birthday celebration was "Provision for the Vision." God spoke on that day that He would send many misfits to the Tabernacle. I knew exactly what God was saying, because at that moment I considered myself as a misfit. As a matter of fact, when I look back, I've been a misfit all of my life.

When you are different, people just don't understand you. As a matter of fact, there were many times when I did not understand myself; but I clearly understand now, it was the calling of God on my life. When God said "Now is the time for the Tabernacle to be formed"; no one wanted to have anything to do with me or the ministry; but the calling of God is irrevocable. Yes, God allowed me to feel like a misfit so I could identify with all other misfits He would send to the Tabernacle. God made me fit for the Kingdom of God, and now uses me to make other misfits fit for His Kingdom.

What I value most about TOPC is the growth. Against all odds, the Lord adds to the church daily such as should be saved (Acts 2:47). Against all odds, the ministry grows spiritually as well as numerically. Against all odds, the ministry has seven associate ministers, and the overseer of Passion for Christ Ministry.

TOPC's mission is to help populate the kingdom of God and to equip a people who cannot be shaken, always battle ready to face the world, walking in the power of the Holy Spirit, walking in integrity and the personality of Jesus Christ for effective Christian living. Against all odds, the mission is being fulfilled.

TOPC's vision is to become a mobile Tabernacle of Prayer to build a worshipping and working community of active parishioners from different ethnic groups and socio-economic levels with a ministry focus on pursuing the un-churched in the Hampton Roads area. Against all odds, the vision is being fulfilled.

Against all odds, on May 3, 2009, God allowed me to fulfill **"Psalm 90:10 KJV, The days of our years are three-score years and ten; and if by reason of strength they be fourscore years, yet is their strength labour and sorrow; for it is soon cut off, and we fly away."**

AGAINST ALL ODDS!!!

2

TESTING THE VISION

"The Lord your God has led you these forty years in the wilderness,

that He might humble you, testing you, to know what was in your heart,

whether you would keep His commandments or not."

(Deuteronomy 8:2, NASB)

When you recognize and accept the call of God on your life, it is usually followed by a feeling of excited anticipation as you realize that you will be used to impact the lives of others. You may be called out by your pastor or singled out by someone and the vision you have is confirmed when that person speaks words which the Holy Spirit has previously spoken within your heart. You are blown away with joy as you hear the message coming from the lips of someone whom you have not shared conversation with about your vision. It is as if they are reading the scroll of God which was fed to you, and it in a way seals that which you may have been unsure of before. It will usually happen unexpectedly; leaving you feeling a sense of confirmation, comfort, and clarity.

My former pastor said once that he used to get so excited when someone would give him "a word from the Lord". Then he realized that the divine message would soon be followed by a test or a trial, and upon that revelation, when someone approached him to "speak a word over his life", he wanted to stop them in their tracks and run the other way! At the time we all laughed, but it wasn't long after that when I began to realize how he felt. His experience played itself out in my own life. It is a fact that "to whom much is given, much is required".

Every product known to man goes through a series of trials, in order to test its quality and expose defects and areas within it, which need to be changed, removed, or strengthened, so that the final product is fit for its intended use. When we are in school, we are tested on that which has been covered in class. These tests evaluate our knowledge, our ability to retain information and apply it to our practical lives. We are evaluated at our workplace, in order to determine if we will be suitable for promotions, based upon the integrity, dependability, and dedication of our performance.

So why should we not expect that one who has been called to such an honorable service--which will enrich and empower the lives of others, also be tested? Oh yes, God equips us with the gifts and desire to do this work, but He takes His chosen ones through a series of tests which will cultivate the heart and mind of His servant. Because of His great love and concern for those whose lives will be impacted, God's front-line soldier must be refined.

Every servant of God must go through "quality control", and be approved by "Inspector Seven", (who is God) in order to be released into their proper role. Along the way you may encounter the following tests. I speak from personal experience.

The Test of Servant-hood:

This test develops faithfulness and loyalty. One cannot lead without first being willing to serve. Let us all remember that Jesus, the Son of God, washed His disciples' feet. This had to be a very dirty job. By doing this, I believe that it showed the disciples that Jesus was totally committed to them. There was nothing He would not do for them. He was also showing them, by example, that in order to lead others to God they must exhibit the love of God in every area.

At the heart of every servant of God is humility. A humble servant will always make a brilliant leader, but a prideful leader will never allow him/herself to be a humble servant. I was heavily tested in this area when I had to care for my disabled father. I had to bathe him, brush his teeth, change his diapers, feed him, dress him, and move him back and forth from his wheelchair and his bed. He would act out against me in anger for the slightest of things, like not cut his toast in the right direction. He would defecate and urinate on me and laugh in my face. He would act out inappropriately in a sexual manner while I was bathing him. He was suffering from mental illness as well as physical affliction. Keep in mind that I was caring for a man who had perpetrated abuse upon me in my childhood and young adulthood, but God had charged me with the task of doing what was right—that is, being there for my father in his time of need.

Although this was a painful and physically/emotionally difficult test for me, I had to go through it. I could have walked away from my father, but the test of servant hood would manifest itself in another way. I could not avoid it if I wanted to move forward in my destiny. You may not have to go through this test in the same manner I did, but you will have to take it at some point. The greatest joy is that once you have taken, and passed this test, you will move forward more equipped and stronger than you were before.

In order to pass the test of servant-hood, God's chosen one must be faithful to Him. This is expressed by time spent with God in reading His Word, and communicating with Him in prayer. You must realize that prayer, in and of itself, is a powerful weapon. Through time spent with God in prayer, you will be equipped with the wisdom, strength, and knowledge of how to proceed in your destiny. This is why the devil fights us so hard in trying to keep us from prayer time. He knows that this acknowledges our dependence on God, and that in turn God will give us the power to fight against the attacks of the enemy.

A proper servant is also completely obedient to the Master. When God speaks, you listen. When He tells you to move, you move without reluctance. When God tells you to stand, you stand. You trust God completely for instruction in every area. We must rely on His guidance for each step we take in fulfilling our destiny. Do what God tells you to do—nothing more, nothing less.

The Wilderness Test:

This test teaches you the ways of the Holy Spirit. Just as Moses was purified for forty years in the desert, this test purifies us. It removes all the ways of the world from within us. All of the things the world views as that which gives us value, power, and popularity are stripped away, as the mind is transformed and renewed by the Word of God. (*"Be not conformed to this world, but be transformed by the entire renewing of your mind." Romans 12:2*) In many ways, this test mirrors the next one I will explain…

The Patience Test:

This test teaches you how to surrender to God. You must learn to completely yield EVERYTHING to God. We often tell God "Lord, all that I have and all that I am I give to you!" But do you really mean that? Remember my beloved, God knows all things, and He examines all things. How long will you wait for Him to fix your bad marriage? How long will you wait for Him to move in your financial situation? How long will you wait for Him to give you a promotion on your job, (or give you a new one)? How long will you wait for Him to draw your children into the Kingdom? How long will you wait for Him to prosper your ministry?

It is not really ME who asks you these questions, it is God. He waits for the core of our heart to surrender, or completely let go of all of the issues we struggle with so that He can do that which we cannot do. He knows if we have let go, that is, He knows when we have put away all of our "back-up" plans. God will even wait until we have exhausted ourselves to the point of complete frustration. He does this not to be mean or spiteful, but because He wants us to realize that we can do NOTHING without Him. God wants all the glory—He wants us to realize that we must wait on Him, (and trust Him) to do the right thing at the right time.

This test causes us to re-examine our spiritual priorities. It causes us to get our eyes off of the natural things and on the things of the Spirit. It teaches us to trust in spiritual things, not natural. The "test of time" will develop and purify your faith in God. God examines our motives and attitudes, and reveals to us the areas which need to be readjusted. It can be painful to look at the "man in the mirror", but we must look at him/her. It is not enough to want to do the right thing for the wrong reason. God realizes our imperfections, weaknesses, and faults and chooses to use us anyway, but He will prune away those "branches" which do not bear fruit or have "rotten berries" so as not to poison anyone else.

Jesus' words in Matthew 7:1-5 deals with us about being judgmental of others. In some translations of these verses it is written, "*How can you tell your neighbor to take the toothpick out of their eye when you have a telephone pole in your own eye*". We must maintain a high level of "teachability" (and I know I just made up a word) but stay with me—we need to remain moldable, and teachable for God to be able to change us, release us, and use us to help others and fulfill our divine destiny. Picture this, if you have a telephone pole in your eye, every time you move you are going to hit someone and cause injury to everyone around you. God wants us to be willing to first recognize that we have that big pole in us and work with Him so that He can remove it before we will be useful to God.

So often we want to have big ministries and help the world, but our "heart posture" is not in the right place—by this I mean that even though we may be on our knees, our heart is not in a submissive position before God. That pole in your eye may be bitterness, anger, pride, envy, un-forgiveness, greed and the list goes on and on. These things must be pruned off, burned off, and removed before God can allow us to completely fulfill all that He has predestined for us to do. When people in the world see us, God wants them to see His image—they should see, at least in part, the characteristics of God when they see us.

Hebrews 12 says that God is "a consuming fire"—that says to me that if we are willing to work with God, He will burn up all that is within us that does not reflect that which gives Him glory. It is a painful process, but shouldn't the ultimate goal of all who profess to love God to be reflections, or as Paul calls us, written, living letters of all that is Christ Jesus? This should be our ultimate goal—when this becomes our goal, God will most assuredly fulfill His promises to us and cause us to fulfill all that we are called to do. All of us in the Body of Christ have a divine call on our lives—your pulpit may be in a church, your backyard fence, or your job place. Wherever it may be it is there waiting on you to take your rightful place. But God will not allow you to take your place knowing that there are things within you that will cause others more pain than good.

The Warfare Test:

This test develops your "spiritual muscles". It's time to grow up, my friends. You see, the devil knows the area of your greatest weakness and he will most definitely attack you at its core. This is when you must learn to exercise the knowledge of the Word that is in you. One of the pieces of the Armor of God is the "Sword of the Spirit" (see Gal. 5:16). The devil cannot stand against the Word of God.

You must speak the Word of God back to the devil when he comes against you. Remember, in Matthew 4:1-10 we read of how after being led into the wilderness by the Spirit, Jesus was tempted by the devil. The Word of God says, "the devil said to Jesus…and Jesus said to the devil". Jesus spoke the Word of God back to the devil—He didn't cower, He didn't think about it, He SPOKE THE WORD OF GOD!!

This is a powerful example of how He Who was the Son of God was led into a "rough, wasteland" for a long time, and then the devil came to Him to tempt Him to do the wrong thing. But Jesus knew what His Father's Word promised Him, and He put the devil in his place by speaking those promises back to him. It is written that after Jesus did this that the devil left him—until a more opportune time. He will come back to us again to bring temptation, but you just put him in his place again.

Remember the words of Jesus as He spoke to the disciples during The Last Supper.

"Simon, Simon, behold, Satan had demanded permission to sift you like wheat, but I have prayed for you, that your faith may not fail, and you, when once have turned again, strengthen your brothers." (Luke 22:31-32, NASB)

These are just a few tests of God's chosen servant. There are many more which try the quality, stamina, fortitude, and resistance of the front-line soldier. But don't give up during the time of testing. You will come out stronger, wiser, more compassionate, and be "spiritually-fit" for our Heavenly Father's use. He will not take you through anything that will cause you to break under the pressure. The "refining fire" will only cause you to emerge as pure gold.

3

THE GIDEON COMPLEX

"…Gideon said to Him 'If now I have found favor

in Your sight, then show me a sign

that it is You who speak with me."

(Judges 6:17, NASB)

This is going to be a very short chapter. You ask "why"? Well my friends, God dealt with me very abruptly on this subject. The "Gideon Complex" is defined by the need for God to constantly confirm and reaffirm the call He has placed upon our lives. I went around this mountain so many times. I want to try to help you avoid piling up mileage in doing the same.

Once God has chosen, anointed, and appointed us to do great things for His glory, it is hard to receive at first. We feel the desire building up within us like a mighty fire which is kindled as each day passes. You want to fulfill this divine appointment so bad you can hardly stand it. You think each new day will offer opportunities for you to exercise the gifts God which has equipped you, and you look for anyone and everyone to share your vision with. But you cannot seem to find anyone to receive you! Confusion builds. Frustration sets in. Then doubt floods your mind like a raging river. What's going on? Where is God?!

I am going to share with you how it all played out for me—I hope it will bless you. First of all, realize that God has not gone anywhere. He is right where He was when He called you into service for Him. This is easy for me to say now, but when I went through this "complex", knowledge of this fact was nowhere to be found in my mind. The only thing that was there was the enemy telling me that I had made this "vision" all up in my mind. He was telling me that I should just give up and go back to living my normal existence just as I was before God "spoke to me".

It was a very difficult time. Even though everything around me and in my mind was telling me that my vision was a lie, there was something deep within me that would not and could not let it go. The passion and desire inside me to fulfill my divine appointment was so strong it would not go away. Yes, the fire would die down for a time, but for some unknown, unexplainable reason, it would always be rekindled. Each time it was rekindled, the fire within me to "do this thing" would burn hotter than ever! And so it went on for years, back and forth, and back and forth—it was sheer torture!

I would go to my church each Sunday hoping to be called out by my pastor. I would visit *different* churches hoping to get a Word from God. I would attend workshops praying to be called forth to the altar and receive confirmation from the Man or Woman of God concerning my call. I spent hours on my face before God praying for Him to send someone to speak a Word over my life. This was usually followed by me attending pity party after pity party, crying buckets of tears pleading with God to answer me.

Then one day God led me to read the story of Gideon. I was intrigued but I still did not get it. Then one Sunday at church, my pastor spoke a message about Gideon. I was amazed, but I still did not get it. Finally, a third time I heard another message about Gideon on a teaching tape—the light bulb came on.

Just as God dealt with Gideon, He dealt with me. He said, *"My daughter, how many times must I speak to you! How many times must I tell you what I want you to do?! You are not deaf or dumb—you know My voice and you know what I have told you! It doesn't matter what others say or do not say! It doesn't matter who approves or who does not approve! I do not have to get the approval of man to choose who I want to choose. I spoke My purpose for your life to YOU, not anyone else! Do not look for anyone else to agree with you over your destiny. What I have ordained, I will pay for—what I have spoken, I will bring to pass! It was etched in the stones of time before the foundation of the world! Now go forth, and stop being pitiful!"*

Well, I guess He told me! And what He has told me I pass on to you. Yes, there will be occasions when God will use a prophet to confirm your call. There may be instances when God uses others to speak a Word over your life. But it will never be anything that you have not heard whispered in the core of your spirit by God first. God will open your eyes and ears to see, hear, and receive your divine assignment. Then He expects you to step out of the boat and walk on the water.

He uses the "the silent times" to prepare you, mold you, purify you, and refine you in order to fully release His power within you. You must utilize your knowledge of the Word of God, wielding the Sword of the Spirit to fight off the powers of the enemy during the testing time.

You do not need a trumpet blast, three angel visitations, and a manifestation of Jesus standing at the foot of your bed, to know that God has called you. You already _know,_ my beloved. Examine your heart. *You already know.*

4

THE JONAH EXPERIENCE

"…And the Lord appointed a great fish to swallow Jonah,

and Jonah was in the stomach of the fish three days and three nights."

(Jonah 1:17, NASB)

Most of us are familiar of the story of Jonah. The first thing most of us remember when Jonah's name is mentioned is when he is swallowed up by the whale. It is perhaps one of the most profound stories recounted in the Old Testament. Jonah, a man used powerfully by God, had to experience a tremendously frightful event in order to fulfill his destiny or divine assignment. He was a great Man of God; however, he had to be humbled/disciplined rather harshly by God. It is truly a fact that once God has chosen you for a specific task, He does not change His mind about it and will see that it is completed—we do not get a vote—God will have His way.

When we read the book of Jonah it is immediately apparent that he had an intimate relationship with our Heavenly Father. In this story of God's loving concern for all people, Nineveh is known as being a great enemy of Israel. Stubborn and reluctant, Jonah represents Israel's jealousy of their favored relationship with God, therefore he was unwilling to share the Lord's compassion with a people whom they considered an enemy. Because of this, Jonah outwardly refused to go to Nineveh to deliver the word of the Lord. It is ironic that a man who loved God so much would rather run from Him, falling into disobedience, than share the compassion of God with his enemies. Jonah had already passed judgment on the people of Nineveh within his heart and wanted God to follow suit, instead of the other way around.

I believe that Jonah's heart was in the right place because of the purity of the passion he had for God. He loved God and wanted everyone else to measure up to that same standard in their love for God. Jonah knew that if Nineveh did not repent for their wicked ways to God, they would suffer utter, total destruction. However he was being prideful in his thinking by assuming that those who were his enemies did not deserve to receive mercy from God. Jonah's motives did not matter to God. Jonah's feelings did not matter to God. The fact that the people of Nineveh were enemies to the people of Israel did not matter to God.

God showers His compassion and mercy upon the believer and the unbeliever. God's love is felt for those who love Him back and those who ignore His love. This may not seem fair to those who have passion for God and share an intimate relationship with Him, but the ultimate call for judgment is not ours. Our responsibility is to continue to grow in our relationship with God and be vessels of His love to all people. I'm getting off course, so let's get back to Jonah.

In the end, God's will was fulfilled, as there was a great storm and Jonah was cast into the sea by frightened sailors on a ship on course for Tar shish. It was then that Jonah was "saved from drowning by being swallowed up by a whale". "Oh boy", Jonah must have thought to himself; "Can this day get any better?!". (smile) First he is on the run from his God-given mission (and I'm sure that Jonah feels a great amount of guilt for being disobedient), he gets aboard a ship full of God-fearing sailors who blame him for the storm that threatens to tear their ship apart and gets thrown into the sea, then he gets swallowed up by a whale! If this doesn't prove that disobedience to God doesn't pay, I don't know what does!

I believe that God used all of these events in order to convince Jonah that He would have His way in the end. God had to allow Jonah to have such bad luck resulting from his own actions that he would finally give in and obey God's command. When Jonah delivered the word of the Lord to the people of Nineveh, it resulted in their repentance and God showed mercy upon them and did not destroy them.

In case you haven't figured it out by now, "The Jonah Experience" involves and is has to with three main issues:

1) Pride

2) Trying to run from your God-given destiny/Disobedience

3) Allowing our flesh to dictate our steps/the message of God

Now I know that when God begins to deal with us about any of these three things, the flesh starts scrambling. People don't like to be told about this, or should I say, reminded of this. I say reminded of this, because most of us know when we are acting in this way deep down in our heart. If one is a believer, saved, and on his/her way to Heaven, we know because the Holy Spirit brings conviction immediately and tells us when we are wrong. Even if one is an unbeliever, they know right from wrong as it relates to anything. Spiritual ignorance is never an excuse for being full of pride and judgmental of others.

Christians who know the Word of God, are well aware of how much God hates pride. He warns in His Word that "pride comes before a fall". Pride lies dormant within everyone. At times pride comes forth and rears its ugly head in various ways. It could take the form of us looking down our nose to someone who comes to church in order to find God. We turn on that "sanctified look of disapproval" when they don't smell of sweet cologne or come dressed as well as we do. We scoot down the aisle to distance ourselves from that person whose eyes look red or clothes are wrinkled, and we automatically assume it is because they have been out partying all night long. Maybe they just got off from a twelve hour shift, or don't have the money buy an iron—what about the red eyes you say? Has anyone heard of eye infections or allergies? Even if they did come straight from partying all night long, a bed of fornication, or have an addiction to drugs and alcohol, have they not come to the right place for deliverance?

Let's face it, none of us are perfect and ALL of us have a past. Your past might not be one filled with any of the above, but God despises self-righteousness, gossip, and judgment. Jesus spent many-a-day in the company of prostitutes, thieves, murderers, and other sinners. He said, "I came for the sick". The church is supposed to be a type of "hospital" for those who are sick in the spiritual realm. People in the world hear about us preach to them of a God Who is loving, merciful, and gracious. How do they have a chance to know Him Whom they *cannot* see if they cannot see His Spirit manifest Himself in us, whom they *can* see? We must share the Good News with all people, whether we believe they deserve to hear it or not.

When you try to deny or ignore fulfilling your destiny, you will always end up in overwhelmingly stressful situations. You will feel as though you are always fighting a battle you cannot win. You will always feel a measure of unhappiness and un-fulfillment. Running from your God-given destiny will always result in your being "swallowed up in the belly of a whale".

The "belly of your whale" may be a job you dread going to everyday, family betrayal/ abandonment, financial ruin, or even man-made prison bars. It doesn't matter how the "belly of your whale" manifests itself, you can only find deliverance, or freedom from it by

God's Hand. Deliverance will only come when God knows you have had enough of being in "the belly" that you will seek Him and His will for your life. God is patient and the Holy Spirit is a gentleman. God will not MAKE you choose the right decision, or His will. He does not change His mind about your call/vision/destiny, but He will not force you to fulfill it. He will, however, allow you to become so unhappy and frustrated that you will seek His guidance to fulfill it.

No matter how you look at it, being in the "belly of your whale" is the result of pride, disobedience, and tolerance of the flesh. The manifestation could be outward, meaning making bad choices, or it could be purely spiritual, meaning one's ignoring the guidance of the Holy Spirit. Either way, the result is never good—not for long anyway. Because we serve a loving God and the fact that His grace and mercy is never-ending, we are given time to turn things around on our own. But if we ignore God too long, He will allow a storm to ravage our circumstances. We can all be thankful that this storm will never end in our being totally destroyed.

God uses the storms in our lives to bring us to our rightful place. That rightful place I'm talking about is intimacy with God, dependence on Him, and fulfillment of our divine destiny. Our arrival to this blessed place is so much bigger than we are—it has more to do with the salvation, deliverance, freedom, and wholeness of others who cannot achieve this any other way or from any other source. It is all linked to God.

5

Do You Have An "Ezekiel Call" on Your Life?

"I am sending you to them who are stubborn and obstinate children,

And you shall say to them, 'Thus says the Lord God'..."

(Ezekiel 2:4, NASB)

I know you may be asking, what exactly is an "Ezekiel call"? Before I explain further, let me first give you some information on who the prophet Ezekiel was and how God spoke to him about his mission for the Kingdom.

Ezekiel's name means "God strengthens". He had a dual role as prophet and priest. Ezekiel was a preacher whose sermons were produced out of a heart of the spiritual welfare of his flock. In the book of Ezekiel chapter one, the Man of God receives his charge (or mission) from God. The prophet says:

> *"As the appearance of the rainbow in the clouds on a rainy day, so was the appearance of the surrounding radiance. Such was the appearance of the likeness of the glory of the Lord. And when I saw it, I fell on my face and heard a voice speaking. Then He said to me, 'Son of man, stand on your feet that I may speak with you!' As He spoke to me the Spirit entered me and set me on my feet, and I heard Him speaking to me. Then He said to me 'Son of man, I am sending you to the sons of Israel, to a rebellious people who have rebelled against Me; they and their fathers have transgressed against Me to this very day. (Ezekiel 1:28, 2:1-3, NASB)*

When God appears to Ezekiel in order to reveal the mission placed upon him, God tells the prophet right away that he is being sent to minister to a stubborn group—a flock of God's children who have rebelled against Him, not listening to their Heavenly Father's words of guidance. In fact, God tells Ezekiel over and over again, that these people will not listen to him, but He also reiterates that the prophet must not be moved by his flock's attitude. God tells Ezekiel that he must be obedient and speak all that he is instructed to say, regardless of how he is received—or rejected.

Ezekiel is instructed to "eat the scrolls", which have been "written on the front and back, and written on it were lamentations, mourning, and woe" (see Ezekiel 2:9). In other words, God was giving the prophet a strong message of destruction, grieving, and sorrow. Not good news, not a "taste-good, feel-good" word of encouragement—not a message that would soothe the flesh, or make the children of Israel want to hear what the prophet Ezekiel had to say or welcome him when they saw him coming. In fact I'll bet they wanted to curse him, scoff at him, and maybe even stone him at first sight! No, it was not an easy mission, to say the least—it probably didn't make Ezekiel feel good, nor did it make him feel a huge sense of enthusiasm in delivering it to his flock. You may not agree with me at first thought, but let us remember that all of the servants God used were mere men and women at the core. They felt all of the same emotions we feel, even though we do not read a lot about it. All who are chosen by God want to be received well, and after all, rejection is hard to deal with on every level—by everyone.

Yet in reading further in the chapters to follow, God tells Ezekiel that he must deliver the message he had been given, without fear and without any adjustment. God charged Ezekiel to deliver the Word of the Lord with conviction, confidence, and clarity. God did not want the message to be watered down, candy-coated, or modified. God was serious about admonishing and chastising the children of Israel because of their disobedience, and He had chosen the prophet Ezekiel to be the one to deliver the Word of correction to them. God later told Ezekiel that He would hold him accountable if he did not say what he was told to say—that the "blood of those who perished would be on his hands"! Wow, can you imagine Ezekiel's feelings when God told him that?! It wasn't enough that he had been charged with delivering a very strong word from God to those who would not listen, but Ezekiel was also told that he must say everything he had been instructed to say or else God would hold *him* responsible for their deaths!

I can imagine the heaviness that Ezekiel must have felt initially, but God knew that He had chosen one who loved Him with every fiber of his being. Because of this, God knew that Ezekiel would be obedient to fulfill his mission because of his great love for God—and because he longed for all of God's children to love Him and wanted them to grow up spiritually. Ezekiel's love for God out-weighed his need for approval of man, and therefore he found fulfillment as he accepted and completed his assignment.

In 2004, as I was spending quiet time with God, I heard the Spirit whispering to me that I had an "Ezekiel call" on *my* life. At the time I had no knowledge of who the prophet Ezekiel was, nor did I know what his mission was for God. Then God led me to read several chapters of the book of Ezekiel, and I have to be honest, what I read scared the daylights out of me! You see, although some of it excited me, being told that my disobedience would result in God holding me accountable for others' ignorance scared me. There was still a part of me that longed to be accepted, honored, and approved by others. It seemed like all throughout my life people ignored me when I spoke. As a young person I was very soft-spoken so some time people said they had a hard time even hearing what I was saying. This concerned me when I answered the call on my life.

I wanted to be able to deliver messages that would be received with joy, thereby resulting in others respecting and loving me. If I was an "Ezekiel-like" servant, much of what I would have to speak would be strong words of conviction, correction, and warnings for disobedience. That's not what folks always want to hear!! That ain't the case *most* of the time!! People want to receive words of encouragement and messages that say how God loves them and wants them to prosper. They want messages that speak prophetically, saying; "Your breakthrough is on the way!". I don't mean to sound funny, I'm just being real—come on, you know what I'm talking about!!

I hate to go there, but I've got to—most pastors today hold back on speaking strong messages of correction to their congregates for fear of losing members and tithes. Uh oh, I stepped on some toes, but I'm being real People! God's people have been allowed to feel comfortable in their sin because they do not hear that confirming word from their spiritual leaders on Sunday morning. I say "confirming word" because the Spirit Who abides within the believer, brings conviction for sin first, God then speaks the same word through the pastor as confirmation. But a lot of times, pastors are not willing to deliver the Word of correction, or they "water it down" in order to not offend anyone. God is not concerned or moved by His children being offended—He is more concerned about us growing up, growing closer to Him, and being all which He has created us to be in this world.

We also must be mindful not to "candy-coat" the Word of God in order to keep membership tallies up, and the collection plate full. In this day and age, the devil is attacking at full force with every sort of tactic, but each subject is addressed in God's Word plainly and concisely. Subjects like sex, homosexuality, and other so-called controversial topics in the religious sect are being danced around by some pastors and God is not pleased by this. Everything is to be done in decency and in order; however these topics must be addressed by the church so that our young people get accurate, spiritual information to nurture their spirit.

Sex is not taboo to God. Perverted sex is taboo to God. The emotions and feelings generated by the flesh in the heat of passion are not sinful when acted out between a husband and wife. God speaks about intimacy in His Word, and there needs to be more teaching within the church concerning this subject and many others—I did not mean to go there, but take it for what it's worth, my beloved.

I am not saying that God doesn't love us or that He is so angry that He is not going to bless us. On the contrary, God is so in love with us that He wants deep, intimate fellowship with us. He wants to bless us; in fact, He has no problem having us prosper abundantly in every area of our lives. But He is also a jealous god, and He will not share His glory with anything or anyone. He will not bless us with anything that He knows will cause us harm or cause us to drift away from Him. Let's be honest here, most of us know that if we had no problems, weaknesses, or issues in our lives we would not feel a need for a deep relationship with God. Unfortunately it is a sad fact that most of us, myself included, would not have received our salvation had it not been for something drastic happening in our lives that woke us up the fact that we needed Jesus.

I have grown a lot in understanding the "Ezekiel call"; first, because I know I have been chosen as such and second, because I have been given a greater level of knowledge of all that it entails. I know that there are many of you reading this book who has this charge as well, so let me help you grow in it—you will accept it with joy and realize the honor you have been given by God.

First, know that God's love and confidence in you is very strong. He knows the heart of all of us, and He knows what is at the core of your heart. He knows that you hold great passion for Him, and He knows that because you are so in love for Him, you desire all to have that same love for Him as well. Because you love God and want others to love Him, you will accept God's Word of God with joy. In Ezekiel chapter three, it says "I ate the scrolls and they tasted as sweet as honey"—when I read this for the first time, God spoke to me saying: "When you read my Word and receive revelation of what I am saying, it makes you feel real good inside doesn't it? You receive it with joy, and you say to yourself 'Oh, that was good!'" I laughed out loud when God spoke that to me, because it was so true! Whenever I received revelation when studying God's Word, I always shouted with joy or began to praise God as I wrote it down.

It didn't matter how strong the revelation was, I accepted the conviction and repented when necessary, while the passion I felt for God grew stronger and stronger. It began to bother me when I encountered other believers who were not allowing their light to shine—the light that distinguishes us from the unbeliever. I just wanted others to really *revere* God in their hearts and have real passion for God. I wanted people to stop "dating Jesus" and "get married to Him".

Dating Jesus means you have a date with Him on Sunday and maybe Wednesday (or whenever you go to Bible Study or other functions), but spend no time with Him in between. When you marry Jesus, you become intimate with Him. You speak with Him every day, several times a day. You consult with Him on everything and you see Him as the Head of your life. You are completely submissive to Him and you allow Him to become one with you in spirit, soul, and body. You become spiritually intimate with Him and He impregnates you with the Holy Spirit, and the seed of your destiny. We need in indwelling of the Holy Spirit, in order to receive guidance, wisdom, and comfort in nurturing the seed of our purpose/destiny, into growing to its full potential.

Although those who share this "Ezekiel call" with me, may share my zeal for delivering the Word, we must also accept the fact that all will not cheer us on. We must realize that there will be few around us to give support, grasp the vision, agree with us in prayer over it, or think what we have been called to do, is actually a God-given mission. In fact you must *look* for people to laugh at you, look at you like you're speaking a foreign language when you tell them about your vision, and even expect some of those closest to you to try to discourage you, and not support you at all, in stepping out to walk in your purpose.

You will be called to speak to congregates who look at you with blank faces, some may walk out while you are speaking, and others may try to make you cut your message short. I have experienced all of the above, and no, it was not easy. The devil tried to make me give up, shut up, and go back to living in the background of life. But the Spirit inside me would not let me rest. He kept on watering the seed of my destiny, and speaking words of conviction about being passive concerning my purpose.

God continuously reminded me what He said about "holding me accountable for the ignorance of others". Why? Because even the Word of God says *"the people perish for lack of knowledge" (see Hosea 4:6)*. When God releases a Word concerning whatever He chooses, it behooves the servant of God to deliver it to whomever He reveals it is for, whether we like it or not. It is not our job to be a "dessert chef" serving up "good, sweet treats" all the time to God's people. The message we are charged with delivering, is a good Word; it is one that will challenge people to grow up in their walk with God. This will result in their being blessed in the end, if they heed the Word they receive. But it is not our concern *or* responsibility whether or not they receive the Word—it is our job to deliver *only*, the ultimate choice is theirs. The responsibility is lifted from us, but we must practice obedience when delivering the Word.

We "Ezekiel-like" servants don't need to even worry about the rejection we may face. God rewards those who diligently seek Him *AND* obey Him. He will make sure you get a glorious reward and will see that you also receive honor for your obedience. God is faithful—all which He has promised, He will bring to pass. But we must do our part. He is not going to do it for you. Most importantly, remember just as God spoke to Ezekiel, He is speaking to all of us saying, ***"Do not fear, for I am with you. Even though they won't listen, when you speak and go, they will know that a prophet has been among them"*** *(see Ezekiel 2:5-6).*

In the beginning of this chapter I wrote that the name "Ezekiel" means "God strengthens". I take this to mean that the one who has an "Ezekiel call" on his/her life will receive supernatural spiritual strength from God. How? You will receive power, renewed anointing and strength through the obedience of pressing past the rejection, disapproval, and stubbornness of those ignoring your message when you release it to them. Each time you exercise obedience in doing what God has called you to do, no matter how it is received, you will gain "toughness", bravery, and renewed determination to go forward in our call. You will become so hardened to needing the approval of others, that you will be more and more compelled to fulfill your God-given assignment. Be encouraged my friends—God is with you. Remember no man can curse whom God has blessed—if God be for you, who can come against you? When God has chosen, anointed, and appointed you, failure is not possible in anything you step out to do.

6

STAYING FOCUSED

"…Fix our eyes on Jesus, the Author and Finisher of our faith…"

(Hebrews 12:2, NASB)

We get so caught up in all that we have yet to "fix" within ourselves, that we often forget that only God can change us. We spend our time worrying, being stressed out, and working in vain to try and achieve that which we perceive to be absolute perfection; feeling that if we can get there, we will finally be "worthy" of being used by God the way He wants to use us. We "dream that impossible dream" of walking in the perfection which only Jesus embodied, in the meantime God is sitting on His throne, tapping His foot and watching the clock—with each minute that ticks by, a soul is lost because we failed to do that which we were called to do.

The fact is my friend, God is well aware of all that we are (as well as all that we are not) when He places a charge to do the work of the Kingdom. Remember, He [on purpose] chooses the things which the world would call weak, to confound the things which the world would call strong; and He chooses [on purpose] the things the world would call foolish, to confound the things which the world would call wise. He does this because He wants all the glory—He wants us, and those in the world, to know that it is *He* that has done the miraculous, *through* us.

If we study and pay close attention to the lives, actions, reactions, and mistakes of the servants in the Word, we will see ourselves in them. All of the servants God used to do the miraculous in the Word had issues—the same issues we struggle with today. Yet they all had passion and determination to fulfill their God-given purpose despite their struggles. This should be our mindset—their example should be our role model.

God wants everyone reading this book to know that He is serious about you fulfilling your destiny—He has had it with the devil's using tactics like gang affiliations, sexual immorality, drug & alcohol addiction, and his sons killing each other—all of the foolishness of his chosen servants getting caught up in the web of the criminal justice (or should I say criminal *injustice*) system! God has sent me to proclaim loud and strong, "*ENOUGH*!!" Enough with generational curses, enough with poverty, enough needless bloodshed, enough with heartbroken mothers shedding tears over their dead and dying sons, *ENOUGH*!!

I speak prophetically to you, and proclaim that God is drawing the bloodline of Jesus over all of the devil's schemes—God says to you; "*You have lost your focus—you have lost sight of who you are and WHOSE you are!!*" God is rebuking the devil *THIS* day and has sent me with a Word to intercept you from venturing down the demonic detour that the enemy has paved for you.

Long ago, a woman named Abigail was sent to King David to do the same—David & his men protected farmers and shepherds during his time in the wilderness. There was a man named Nabal (whose name means "fool") and he had a wife named Abigail—David & his men had guarded Nabal's family & all he owned all night long, and at harvest time, a great party was in full swing —in return for their labor, all David wanted was some food & drink for himself and his men . Nabal denied even knowing David and sent a message by David's men, basically telling David which part of Nabal's anatomy he could kiss. This angered David—frustration took over, and vengeance filled his heart. Abigail heard her husband's response, and took food and drink to David herself. She also pleaded for David to have mercy upon her and her family. By doing this she "intercepted" Satan's detour. For all of you, I have been sent to you as *ABIGAIL*!

Many of us have lost our focus, this is why I want to share what God has taught me about the "reflection" you see or what you perceive about yourself. Of course when we think of the word "reflection" we immediately think of that which we see when we look into a mirror. I would like you to expand your interpretation of the word "reflection". Reflection can be perceived as: A mirror image, a consideration, a likeness, or a way of thinking.

So when thinking about these references, I ask you, when you look at your reflection, what do you see? When God created Adam and Eve, he also placed within them a "reflection" or a likeness—in fact it is written that "when God created man he was created in His own likeness".

As you consider your "reflection", I want you to also to think about something we often do not consider—something we often think is very insignificant—that is, THE POWER OF YOUR WORDS!! The Word of God gives us strong warning about the tongue—it says, *"life and death are in the power of the tongue; from the same tongue spring blessings and curses"*. This not only pertains to what we say about others, but it also pertains to our own lives and what we say about ourselves.

What we see and say about ourselves, affects the "reflection" that gazes back at us when we look through the mirror of our "soul man"; that being our mind, will, and emotions. The "reflection" of the soul controls that which guides the mind (or that which we think about ourselves), our will (or that which we do), and our emotions (or that which we feel). How you perceive or receive the "likeness" within you, affects or guides everything you do, think, and ultimately achieve.

God led me to research several powerful men in the Bible and ask you to look at their "reflection", or their "likeness, way of thinking, and personal considerations. These men are Abraham, Esau & Jacob, Joseph, Moses, and David. I know you are going to see yourself in at least one of these men. It will change how you see yourself. You will realize that there is much more to what you see in your "reflection" –you will realize that God has given you all that you need to bring your destiny into clear focus. It will (in a sort of trickle-down way) redefine the destiny of your children.

Like it or not, our children see themselves through us. What we believe, they believe. What we do and think, they do and think. What we strive to achieve will affect what they feel and how they determine their ability to achieve.

Sooo let's take a look at Abraham, twins Esau & Jacob, Joseph, Moses, and David.

All of these powerful men of God had several things in common—they all had issues. Don't frown at me like that—let me remind you that even though they were divinely chosen, anointed, appointed, and used by God to do great, miraculous, and powerful things, they were first MEN—MORTAL MEN, LIVING IN MORTAL FLESH!! What issues you ask? Well, insecurity, pride, impatience, lust, thievery, and anger just to name a few!

At times we forget that the servants of God were mere men and women with some of the same hang-ups, frustrations, and temptations we have today. Satan has been on the scene from the time of Adam and Eve, and he has been about his work non-stop from that day to this.

In the book of Genesis chapters 12 through 17 we read about the destiny of Abraham. Abraham, his name at the time being Abrahm, was commanded by God to leave his father's house and go to a land which the Lord would show him. God speaks to Abrahm giving him a seven-fold promise: 1) I will make you a great nation, 2)I will bless you, 3) I will make your name great, 4) I will make you a blessing, 5) I will bless those who bless you, 6) I will curse those who curse you, and 7) In you all the families of the earth will be blessed.

Along the way, he hooked up with his cousin Lot, and there came a time when he and Lot had to make a choice about who would inhabit or take ownership of a very prospering area of land. Abrahm gave Lot first choice, and of course he chose the most fruitful area. Abrahm could've been mad and argued with him, but he graciously told Lot he could have the land.

Not long after that the Lord spoke to Abrahm again. God asked Abrahm to look to the north, the south, the east, and the west. In other words, God told Abrahm to look around him. He asked Abrahm, "What do you see?", then God made him a promise that all that his eyes could see, He would give to him and his descendants forever.

Many years after these promises were made to Abrahm by God, the Lord appeared to him again, in order to establish or seal the covenant with him. At this time, God changes Abrahm's name to Abraham, as God defines his "reflection" saying; "For I will make you the father of many nations." The key words here are "many years after these promises were made". We often think when we receive a word from God (directly or indirectly), it will come to pass immediately. This is more often NOT the case, my friends. God "tests" our faith in receiving and believing that which has been spoken.

Let's talk about Esau & Jacob: twins born to Isaac, God's promised son to Abraham.

Jacob's name means "to grasp the heel; the swindler". The story of these two brothers is a sad but familiar one; one brother steals the birthright of the other through fooling his blind dying father. Perhaps the saddest part of this act is that Jacob is prompted to do it by his own mother!

How often have any of you felt that what was rightfully yours has been stolen from you by someone very close to you—and how many of you have felt that others close to you (family or otherwise) encouraged them to betray you?! This is a hurtful thing, and it is a hard thing to forgive. We find ourselves filled with bitterness and we distance ourselves from family or the ones who have betrayed us. But let us remember that the story of Jacob's betrayal of his brother Esau does not end there. Now there is a lot of history in between but I'm going to cut to the chase.

Jacob, years later, arrives at the crossroads of his destiny. There comes a time when Jacob sends his family ahead of him to their new land, and he stays behind. It is written that Jacob builds a fire at nightfall, and then receives a visitor. A divine visitor—and it's rumbling time! Jacob struggles with "an angel of the Lord all night long". God asks Jacob "how long will you strive with Me". Jacob's response is "I will not let you go until you bless me!" In other words, Jacob was sayin, "I hope you packed a lunch 'cuz we gonna be here a while!" Jacob had some nerve!! Jacob refused to let go because he knew God had his destiny in His hands.

Well we know that our God is a loving, merciful, gracious, and awesome God. God makes a new covenant with Jacob and He changes His name to Israel, which means "he struggles with God". Does that sound like anyone you know? Oh yes, we struggle with God on a regular basis! It is by no mistake that we are called the "children of Israel".

Now even though Jacob (now renamed "Israel"), has had a divine visitation and knows that his destiny has been "redefined", he still lives in fear of the wrath of his brother Esau whom he has betrayed. But upon meeting Esau, he is astounded by his brother's reception.

It is written that Esau beholds the anointing upon his brother Jacob. Esau embraces his brother and kisses him, and confirms that God has done a work in him. Jacob blesses his brother Esau.

Moses—Because of Pharaoh's death decree, his mother placed precious baby Moses in a river basket to find his destiny. Ironically, Moses was adopted by the very family that put a "hit" on his life. Being raised by the Egyptians enabled Moses to become acquainted with every area of their way of life. Even though he had no outward evidence of his true heritage, there was something on the inside of him that "reflected" a different "likeness" than that of being an Egyptian. This caused him to act out of season, and after killing a man, he fled from his home.

God purified Moses those 40 years on the back side of the wilderness—but Moses still did not forget what he learned about living in the house of the Pharaoh. Sometimes God will have you in a "displaced" spot for a season—it could be your job, a difficult relationship, or something else—but time spent in this "displaced" spot will equip you with the strength, wisdom, and skills needed to help you fulfill your destiny. Moses knew how Pharaoh would react to him when he returned, and he knew how the children of Israel would react as well, when he told them that God had sent him to be their deliverer.

Maybe this is why Moses' insecurity came forth at that encounter with God at the burning bush. Remember how he kept reminding God why he could not do what God was telling him to do? How many times have you reminded God about all the things that are wrong with you, all your shortcomings, all your failures, and all the reasons why you cannot fulfill what God is telling you to do in regards to your destiny?

God asked Moses a question that day at the burning bush—He asked Moses, "What do you have in your hand?" In other words, what do you have that I have already given you? Of course most of you probably know the rest of the story of that encounter. God tells Moses that by the "staff in his hand" God will enable Moses to do great and awesome things. It is by this same staff that Moses held up at the edge of the Red Sea, and the children of Israel stood in utter astonishment as God parted the waters allowing them to cross over on dry land.

Joseph was known as the dreamer. This young man knew what his destiny would be at a very young age. He accepted it with joy and he thought others would be happy for him...maybe. He shared with his brothers that God told him he would one day be king. He told them this, thinking maybe they would share his excitement—or maybe he felt just a twinge of pride and wanted to brag about it. He never thought they would react the way they did.

He was kidnapped by his own brothers, thrown into a pit, fished out of that pit, sold into slavery, later thrown into prison on a bogus charge of attempted rape, but all the while he remained diligent in flexing the muscle of his natural ability to interpret dreams. This resulted in his release from prison and later he took his rightful place as king. In spite of the betrayal, accusations, imprisonment, and persecutions, his mind was set on fulfilling his destiny.

Did he feel hurt by the rejection and scornful betrayal of his family? *YES!* Did he feel anger for spending years in a dirty, stinking prison surrounded by criminals on a trumped up charge?? *YES!!* Did he ever question God over these things, because above all things, his imprisonment was the result of him denying the sexual advances of the FINE wife of his boss because of his love and reverence for his GOD?! **YES!!!**

But Joseph did not allow any of these feelings to douse the fire that burned within him to fulfill his destiny. The "reflection" within him was stronger and brighter than the counterfeit "likeness" the devil tried to impose upon him.

And finally David, oh poor David! He was totally forgotten and disregarded by his own father Jesse when Samuel came to his house to anoint a successor for Saul. David was the youngest, the smallest of all of his brothers, and the one with the dirtiest job in the house—tending to the livestock in the field.

David—laughed at when he stepped forward to confront Goliath, yet he was the only able to kill him with a sling and one single stone. David—called forth to comfort Saul by playing his music, but later hated and hunted by Saul and his army. David—finally king, but gave into temptation and lust when he couldn't stop watching Bathsheba being bathed by her handmaidens. Can you see him?

A mighty king, warrior, admired by all, standing every night on that tower, cowering and peeping, waiting to get a glimpse of Bathsheba's goodies all lathered up. *Shame, shame!* Kinda' sounds like some anointed, charismatic, men and women of God sitting in silence at that computer all night long pulling up those porn sites or all up in those chat rooms you know you ain't got NO business being in—uh oh, I'm gonna leave that alone!

Back on track, David—sends this woman's poor husband out to the battle line knowing full well he will be killed—all so he can have her for himself. Together, they conceive a child—then the child becomes gravely ill. David mourns the entire time—grieves bitterly. David fasts and prays, lying prostrate before God until the child dies, then David repents before God, and takes up where he left off. God allows David to fulfill his destiny. *WOW!!!*

Abraham, Moses, Esau, Jacob, Joseph, and David—did I hit your house yet? Did you find yourself in any one of their stories? My guess is yes. God says in His Word: The gifts and calling of God are irrevocable. Once God has assigned a job for you to do, He does not change His mind about it. Once God has equipped you with gifts in order to fulfill your destiny, He does not take them back. No one but YOU can stop God's best from being fulfilled in your life.

The thing is: *IT AIN'T ABOUT YOU!!* It's about those who are waiting for you to walk in your destiny. Their souls hang in the balance waiting for your gifts to impact their lives. Readjust your eyesight—ask God to bring your "reflection" into clear focus. I want to emphasize that although I have highlighted the lives of men in this message, the message crosses the gender barrier.

God placed His mark upon me as He formed me in my mother's womb, but I was born with a "death stamp" on my head. I was conceived in 1962, a time of great racial tension— born as a result of a romance between a 17 yr old white girl and an 18 yr old black man. I was supposed to be aborted because of the shame my birth brought to my birth mother's southern Baptist household. But she gave me up to be adopted, and although I was raised with much in the material realm, I was also subjected to years of childhood abuse, rape, addiction, rejection, domestic abuse, persecution, ridicule, and hardship. But God used all of these things to mold me, shape me, and restore the "reflection" of the "likeness" within me so that I could discover and walk in my destiny. I now ask you all of the questions He asked me along the way:

I ask you, as God asked Abraham, "***What do you see?***"

I ask you as God asked Moses, "**What do you have that God has already given you?**"

I ask you as God asked Jacob, "**How long will you wrestle with God?**"

I ask you as God asked David, "**How long will you mourn?**"

And I tell you as Joseph told his brothers, "**What the enemy meant for your harm, God meant for your good**".

We cannot be moved or deterred by family, friends, or even church folk. Believe me, the enemy will use all of those close to us to distract us, discourage us, persecute and use condemnation in order to keep us from moving forward in fulfilling our destiny. I experienced all of this when I stepped out in ministry.

In fact I began to experience it from the point that I accepted Jesus Christ as my Savior. I *continue* to fight against the personal attacks by the enemy using those closest to me, and have accepted the fact that I will forever be on that demonic hit list. If you are passionate about working on the front line in God's army, you will have to face the same. Remain comforted and encouraged however, always holding on to God's unchanging hand because He is with you.

Conclusion

"For I am confident of this very thing,

that He who began a good work in you will perfect it

until the day of Christ Jesus."

(Philippians 1:6, NASB)

One of my favorite songs is "I Know the Plans I Have for You". One verse says,

"I know the plans I have for you,

I know just what you're going through,

So when you don't know what tomorrow holds

And yesterday is through

Remember, I know the plans I have for you."

In conclusion, let me say that remembering that just as God impregnated you with the vision or purpose for your life, you must always remember that God, and only God, can bring it to fruition. It doesn't matter how talented, how educated, or how naturally gifted you are, God must be in the driver's seat of your destiny. He knows the pathway which leads to you fulfilling your purpose, and He will not fail. He has the roadmap which outlines the design of how you will reach your desired end. He gives us the gift of the indwelling of the Holy Spirit in order to receive instructions, comfort, wisdom, and guidance, but the Holy Spirit is a gentleman. He will not force you to make right decisions—He gives gentle, quiet instruction but He ultimately waits for us to exercise our free will in making the right decision. God will allow us to have our way at times, knowing full well that we do not know what we are doing. He allows us to run into detours, roadblocks, and dead ends until we get to the point of exhaustion and let Him take the steering wheel again. He does this so that we come to the realization that we need Him in every way and cannot do anything without Him.

This may seem cruel but quite frankly most of us will not fully recognize how much we need God until we make a huge mess of things. We wind up sitting in a big pile of rubble brought down by our believing that we know it all. God shows us our purpose (in part) and we take off running thinking we can make it happen on our own. We run into brick wall after brick wall and end up hurt, frustrated, and at times angry, because we refuse to accept the fact that we made the mess ourselves. We want to blame the devil, we want to blame others, and we want to wallow in self-pity. How can I say this with such blatant certainty? Because I have the battle scars to prove it. I have been there, done that, and have boxes of T-shirts to show for it. I am simply trying to save you from the same fate.

God does not appreciate "backseat drivers". Just as we get angry when we are in the driver's seat with our minds set on getting to our destination and someone in the back seat is trying to tell us which way to go, God feels the same way. I believe He gets frustrated with us when we try to tell Him how to get us where we are trying to go. Being a "backseat driver" with God involves and is motivated by pride and the flesh. We must remember that the flesh often has a mind of its own controlled by selfish motives. The flesh has to be crucified and motives must be purified. It is a matter of using restraint, exercising humility, and utilizing self-control.

Trying to fulfill your God-given assignment cannot be done without God being the Head of the plan. He gave you the assignment, and He must (and will) see that you complete it. He will bless you abundantly with the tools, the courage, the guidance, the wisdom, and the abundant rewards for your labor. Trust Him to lead you every step of the way. Trust Him to give you divine appointments, and shower you with honor on each level you conquer. Be not afraid, for He Who has called and chosen you will protect you from your enemies. No devil in hell and no man/woman on earth, can keep you from what God has predestined for you to have and to do. It was written in the divine stones of time before you ever came into existence. God does not change His mind, and He does not take back the gifts He has given to you.

Make up your mind this day that you are going to be determined to fulfill your destiny. There are souls hanging in the balance depending on you. Fulfilling your purpose is so much bigger than you, so get over yourself. God loves you, and He loves those who are waiting for you to minister life to them. You are more than able regardless of your weaknesses, your self-perceived failures, and the past.

I will leave you with the words of the Apostle Paul stated in Romans 8:36-37 (NASB):

"'Just as it is written, For Your sake we are being put to death all day long;

We were considered sheep being led to be slaughtered' But in all these things we overwhelmingly conquer through Him Who loved us."

I pray that this book has blessed, encouraged, and inspired you to press on with unfailing determination to pursue and fulfill your destiny. Your vision is the seed which God implanted within you. Do not rest until you have completed your mission. You will enjoy such an inner peace and fulfillment which cannot be obtained any other way. The greatest reward will be when you meet our Heavenly Father face to face. He will look at you smiling with pride and say to you, *"Well done my good and faithful servant".* God bless you, my brothers and sisters.

Evangelist, Yolanda Grace Lee-Jones

About the. Author:

    Yolanda Grace Lee-Jones is a resident of Chesapeake, Virginia. She is an alumnus of North Carolina A & T State University. Yolanda is married to Rodney A. Jones, Sr., and they have two daughters, Brianna Nicole & Treasure Imani Jones.   She received her license as an evangelist in August 2007. Yolanda is the author of <u>Redemption of Grace</u> (which is her autobiography), and her first children's book <u>The House that Jesus Built.</u> She is currently working on two more books: <u>Holding On to the Vision </u>which will be released in October 2009, and <u>Lest the Lord Builds the House </u>(release date – April 2010). She is also a gospel flutist.

    Yolanda received Jesus Christ as her personal Lord and Savior at the age of 37.   Shortly after her rebirth, God impregnated her with a vision to reach out to those on the same dark road to nowhere she was on when He stepped into her life. Thus, in 2008 Passion for Christ Ministries was born.

    Passion for Christ Ministries is also a mobile ministry, as Yolanda carries her message via music as well as the spoken Word to various churches and venues.

For more information, contact:

Passion for Christ Ministries

P. O. Box 6193

Chesapeake, VA 23323

(757) 737-0560